Aesthetics and Politics: Two Leading Bhojpuri Artists

Sandeep Rai

First Published in 2020

Becomeshakespeare.com

One Point Six Technologies Pvt Ltd
123, Building J2, Shram Seva Premises,
Wadala Truck Depot, Wadala (East),
Mumbai 400037, India
T: +91 8080226699

Wordit Art Fund helps deserving authors publish their work by providing monetary support. To apply for funding, please visit us at www.BecomeShakespeare.com

ISBN - 978-93-90543-50-2

Preface

Bhikhari Thakur through his plays and songs and Gorakh Pandey through his poems and songs portray everyday life and social dimensions of Bhojpuri society between the period of the two world wars and post colonial times. Bhikhari Thakur has beautifully done this through his unique cultural form called 'Bidesia'.This text is an improvisation of my M.Phill thesis in sociology done at Delhi School of Economics, titled 'A Sociological Analysis of Bhikhari Thakur and Gorakh Pandey's works'. Locating their literature, plays, poems and songs, in post colonial paradigm, this book is an attempt to view the reflections of the concepts of Aesthetics and Politics in both their works.

This book has outlined the spaces in contemporary rural social structure. It is worth mentioning that the department of Sociology, Delhi School of Economics where I got the chance to do this research and my teachers, profs Nandini Sundar, Anand Chakravarti and Dr. Anuja Agrawal and Dr. Rabindra Ray taught and guided me so well to be able to comprehend and apprehend, speculate and specify the conviction and caprice of 'Aesthetics and Politics' in the literary and artistic production of Bhikhari Thakur and Gorakh Pandey. Repetitions of section of my argument occur in order to stress on the vitality of the flow of the previous defence.

Acknowledgements

To Mamma who becomes my mother countless times a day. To the Department of Sociology, Delhi School of Economics where I was able to become familiar with the area of my studies, collect materials and carry out my research. To Prof. Alok, who has taught, helped and guided. To Awanish Bhaiya, who has been a true moral support and I thank him specially to have helped me devise the title of this book.

To Dr. Rabindra Ray for his encouragement, support and incredible faith in me. I thank him for challenging me all the time to do my best and for helping me through my most uncertain moments. Above all, I am grateful to him for helping me complete this project successfully.

To Dr. Anuja Agrawal for giving me invaluable advise.

To Dr. Joyoti Gupta, who was there as one huge intellectual support and who gave me many interesting material to read. I am very thankful to my teachers Prof. Nandini Sundar and Prof. Anand Chakravarti who still teach me over phone. I also thank Dr Shahana and Mr. Sanjay Verma who have taught me at undergraduate level but they still suggest and clarify when it has been seventeen years since i passed out from Kirori Mal College. I am grateful to Ameeya Bhai and Shubhadeepta for being there at my disposal all the time while staying more than a thousand kilometers away.

To the friends who were not directly involved with this M Phil book but were there to make my research and life in Delhi School of Economics a memorable experience.

To Tathagatan with whom I engaged in long sociological discussions.

I am very obliged towards my Father, younger brother Sarvesh and nephew Mandeep for their patience and support. I am thankful to Vivek for helping me in edits and corrections and for his technological aid .My heartiest regards to Vivekanad Bhaiya for proving an academic guardian. I am extremely obliged to my buddies and seniors of Sanik School Ghorakhal for granting and ensuring financial support all through. At last but not the least, I am indebted to BecomeShakespeare.com in general, Pranali and Shreyas in particular.

Contents

Introduction

This book is an exercise to explore the relationship between society and literature, particularly through the works of Bhikhari Thakur and Gorakh Pandey, popular Bhojpuri[1] writers of the 19th and 20th centuries respectively. In Thakur's work, I look at his plays and songs, while in Pandey's work I look at his poetry and songs. These works have often been seen as revolutionary and resistant towards the ideologies of the dominant class. Within Marxian theories (as we shall identify in the following chapters), a dominant ideology, is a term synonymously used with concepts such as shared belief systems, ultimate values, and common culture, as the mainstay of social order in advanced capitalist societies. The argument assumes that, in class-stratified societies,

---

[1] The Bhojpuri region is a cultural entity that transcends political borders. This area comprises the eastern part of Uttar Pradesh and the western part of Bihar in India. In the north, it reaches across the river Ganges and past the Nepal frontier, up to the lower ranges of the Himalayas, from Champaran to Basti. In the south, it crosses the Sone River and covers the great plateau of Chotanagpur, where it finds itself in contact with the Bengali of Manbhum, the Oriya of Singhbhum, and the scattered tribal languages of the Chotanagpur plateau. The area covered by Bhojpur is some fifty thousand square miles; more than 15 per cent of the total Indian population speaks Bhojpuri.

the ruling class controls the production of ideas as well as material production. It propagates a set of coherent beliefs which dominate subordinate meaning systems and, as a consequence, shapes working-class consciousness in the interests of the status quo. A dominant ideology functions to incorporate the working class into the society of the ruling class, thereby maintaining social cohesion. The works of Thakur and Pandey have been seen to resist this very false consciousness, offering a critique to the material structure of society and also the existing class relations.

I argue that, the works of these authors fall rather in the realm of agitation propaganda, an idea borrowed from the Russian *Agitprop* and *Proletkult* strategies but gain popularity primarily through their aesthetic qualities. Proletkult is a portmanteau or combination of 'proletarskaya kultura'[2], Russian for 'proletarian culture'. It was a movement active in the Soviet Union from 1917 to 1925 to provide the foundations for what was intended to be a truly proletarian art devoid of bourgeois influence. Its main theoretician was Alexander Bogdanov (1873-1928) who saw the proletkult as a third part of a trinity of revolutionary socialism. Whereas the unions would attend to the proletariat's economic binterests and the

---

[2].   http:.en.wikipedia.org/wiki/Proletkult

communist party, their political interests, the Proletkult would look after their cultural and spiritual life.

Agitprop on the other hand is a political strategy in which the techniques of agitation and propaganda are used to influence and mobilize public opinion. Although the strategy is common, both the label and an obsession with it were specific to the Marxism practiced by communists in the Soviet Union. The term originated in Bolshevist Russia. In fact, the term propaganda in the Russian language simply meant 'dissemination of ideas'[3]. In the case of agitprop, the ideas to be disseminated were those of communism, including explanations of the policy of the Communist Party and the Soviet state. In other contexts, propaganda could mean dissemination of any kind of beneficial knowledge, e.g., of new methods in agriculture. Agitation meant urging people to do what Soviet leaders expected them to do; again, at various levels. In other words, propaganda was supposed to act on the mind, while agitation acted on emotions, although both usually went together, thus giving rise to the cliche 'propaganda and agitation'. The term agitprop gave rise to agitprop theatre, a highly-politicized leftist theatre originated in Europe of 1920s-1930s, spreaded to America as well, with plays of Bertolt Brecht being a notable example. Artists and actors performed simple plays, passing through

------

3.   http:.en.wikipedia.org/wiki/Agitprop

villages and broadcasted propaganda. Gradually the term agitprop came to describe any kind of leftist politicized art.

The twin strategies of agitation and propaganda were originally elaborated by the Marxist theorist Georgy Plekhanov (1898), who defined propaganda as the promulgation of a number of ideas to an individual or small group and agitation as the promulgation of a single idea to a large mass of people[4]. Expanding on these notions in his pamphlet 'What Is to Be Done?' (1902),

Vladimir Lenin stated that the propagandist, whose primary medium is print, explains the causes of social inequities such as unemployment or hunger, while the agitator, whose primary medium is speech, seizes on the emotional aspects of these issues to arouse her/his audience to indignation or action. Agitation is thus the use of political slogans and half-truths to exploit the grievances of the public and thereby to mould public opinion and mobilize public support. Propaganda, by contrast, is the reasoned use of historical and scientific arguments to indoctrinate the educated and so-called enlightened members of society.

---

[4]   Agitprop. Encyclopedia Britannica. 2009. Encyclopaedia Britannica Online. 25 Sep. 2009 <http:.www.britannica.com/EBchecked/topic/9224/agitprop>.

My basic concern throughout the research has been to point out this simultaneous aesthetic, agitational and propagandist dimension of socio-political literature. This assertion is elaborated through the very understanding of the terms 'politics' and 'aesthetics' forwarded in this thesis. Politics according to Jacques Ranciere (2005) is the struggle of an unrecognized party for equal recognition in the established order. politics, he argues itself is not the exercise of power or struggle for power. It is first of all the configuration of a space as political, the framing of a specific sphere of experience, the setting of objects rosed as 'common' and of subjects to whom the capacity is recognized to designate these objects and discuss about them. Politics first is thus the conflict about the very existence of that sphere of experience. Moreover, aesthetics is bound up in this battle, because the battle takes place over the image of society, what it is permissible to say or to show. I use the term aesthetic here in a sense close to the Kantian idea of 'a priori forms of sensibility' (Kant, 1900), referring :o the concepts of space and time as logically necessary conditions for there to be any experience at all. Thus, I see literature as both a matter of art and taste and also fundamentally a matter of time and space. It deals with time and space as forms of configuration of our 'place' in society.

This is the manner in which it is possible to understand the propagandist impulse in the aesthesis of literature.

According to A.P. Foulkes (1983), any propaganda has cultural, social and historical conditions within which it is produced and its recognition depends upon the relative viewpoint of the person observing it. Because of this elusiveness, the propagandist cannot be identified on all occasions. One of the ways in which Jacques Ellul (1973) defines propaganda is by looking at its agitation motive. He asserts that the propaganda of agitation is usually subversive and oppositional. It may seek to overthrow an established order, but may equally be used to address psychological barriers of habits, beliefs and judgments. At the same time, propaganda has an integration effect that produces inertia and conformity to obtain stable behavior. The effects of propaganda can therefore be ineffective because it strives for a spontaneous transformation of society, such that they simultaneously hold a revolutionary potential to change a society but also very subtly maintain the status quo. Thus we find negotiations between dominant and at the same time opposing values and ideologies of society. Accordingly, I argue that the works of Pandey and Thakur, in spite of being resistant to the dominant ideologies, fall within the realm of propagandist literature and also gain popularity because they carry an aesthetic appeal. I accordingly restage the radical writing movement in Bhojpuri literature as an aesthetic movement, in which the practices of women, labour and the marginalized were framed - primarily around the incapacity to voice their experience.

Such a discussion on the relationship between literature and society is multifaceted and has been discussed by literary scholars and sociologists alike. Broadly four characterizations of this relationship can be found: 1) that literature reflects society, i.e. it adheres to or gets generated through the dominant norms of society, 2) that literature influences society or it does not adhere to the prevalent norms and is seen as radical within the existing society. These are often known as resistance literature. Resistance literature is considered as an important factor in the development of political consciousness among subjugated people, 3) that literature functions to maintain or justify the social order, and in effect exerts social control. It often falls in the realm of propaganda art and 4) literature negotiates its way between the three and in the process gains popularity and mass appeal. All four notions ultimately emphasize upon the reciprocal interaction between literature and society.

In this book, there is a particular focus on the third and fourth categories as here we find the motivation for presenting the major themes of this analysis. These themes are set against the backdrop of Marxian Literary Theory, which opened up during the 1920s as part of larger Cultural Studies[5]. The tendency of classical Marxism is to view culture as consisting of so many forms of consciousness which are although viewed as depending upon the material process of economic production and are deprived of any autonomous sphere of determinacy or effectiveness that is distinctively their own. The present analysis takes up the literary theory of Marxism, the emphasis of which is upon the themes of conflict in society. According to this model, literature can be seen as a result of the engagement between base and superstructure, such that the products of literary culture further the interest of capitalism and bourgeois ideologies. Moreover, the receiver of the text is interpreted as passive before these literary devices. These devices are seen to play an important role in influencing public opinion in favour of dominant ideologies, through propagandas.

However, one of the most significant directions taken by work in the sociology of literature in the past two decades has been the reconceptualization of readers as creative

5. [5]There have been several other commonly identified schools of literary theory which have reflected these various themes have existed in the form of for instance, cultural studies (which emphasises the role of literature in everyday life); formalism (which analyses, interprets and evaluates the inherent features of a text. It refers to the inquiry of the form rather than the content of the works of literature); post-colonialism (which focuses on the influence of colonialism in literature); structuralism and post-structuralism (which explain and respectively critique the 'rationality' in culture through linguistic models); gender studies (which focuses on themes of gender relations) and so on.

agents rather than passive recipients of what authors write. Sociologists have embraced European 'reception aesthetics[6]' as a way to understand the construction of literary meaning. Proponents of reception aesthetics argued that the reader never comes to a text as a blank slate. Social scientists have readily reflected upon the different understandings and expectations that different groups or categories of readers bring to a single text. Authors will try to steer the process-every text has an 'implied reader' (Iser i974)-but cannot control it.

Reception aesthetics succeeded in transforming the research agenda in the sociology of literature, in part because it interacted with another theoretical development that was taking place among students of popular culture, one which accorded significant meaning-making ability to people themselves. Where mass culture theorists and hegemony arguments conceptualized the recipients of mass-produced cultural products as rather hapless, newer voices contended that people were more

---

[6.] Bricolage is a term used in several disciplines, among them the visual arts and literature, to refer to the construction or creation of a work from a diverse range of things which happen to be available, or 2 work created by such a process. The term is borrowed from the French word bricolage, from the verb bricoler - the core meaning in French being, 'make creative and resourceful use of whatever materials are to hand"; in contemporary French the word is the equivalent of the English do it yourself. A person who engages in bricolage is a bricoleur.

like 'bricoleurs'[7], making meanings out of whatever was available to them. Moreover, these meanings often subverted the power relations presented in the content of the cultural object.

This view was politically attractive because it respected previously ignored writings genres like regional literature, poetries and texts. These were however reinterpreted as symbols of working class assertiveness, consumed by groups lacking social privilege and cultural capital; in these genres it found the sources of a certain resistance. Indeed, it is then possible to understand the works of Thakur and Pandey within the context of the Russian *Prolethult* and *Agitprop* strategies.

Taking off from the above assertions, One can understand literature as more than merely instruments of dominant bourgeois ideologies. In fact, it locates the processes which enable socio-political literature to be seen in the following manner:

1.   As opposed to the arguments forwarded by the Marxian Literary Theory, it is possible to see

---

7.   Reception theory is a version of reader response literary theory that emphasizes the reader's reception of a literary text. (Also called audience reception.)In literature, it originated from the work of Hans-Robert Jauss in the late 1960s. Reception theory was at its most influential during the 1970s and early 1980s in Germany and USA (Fortier 132), amongst some notable work in Western Europe.

literature as moving away from the dominant bourgeois ideologies. Thus texts, poetries and other forms of writings can be seen as resisting the false consciousness generated by the dominant classes.

2. Furthermore, it is possible to take literature as an enterprise of aesthetics, so that it can be analysed and experienced purely in terms of its entertainment or pleasure value. The aesthetic criteria on which such judgements are based are however not always clearly established.

3. By looking at the writings that have been often understood as resistant and carrying the potential to change mentalities and thereby societies, literary art can also be understood as propagandist. I argue that these radical writings, rather than reflecting a process of change or challenging the dominant values, end up propagandising the issues at hand. Moreover, this propaganda bases itself upon the very aesthetic value of art, which is often denounced by Marxist writers.

4. Finally, literature necessarily reflects ideas about the way in which a society is organized. It reflects the social influences of the authors and the means by which their literary products reach

an audience. It tells us how the sociohistorical context (defined by historical time, economic and political structure, social stratification, and cultural orientation) influence the style and content of the authors' works.

In this attempt, one can look the case of Bhojpuri literature, specifically in the works of Thakur and Pandey where the themes of resistance, aesthetics, propaganda and societal structures get reflected. In fact, their work employs both Agitprop and Proletkult strategies. Thakur who was immensely popular as a ballad singer in Bihar and the Bhojpuri-speaking region of Uttar Pradesh of this past century, wrote about themes ranging from patriotism to social issues. He also attempted to awaken anti-colonial feelings among the masses during the British Raj. Known for his play i.e. 'Bidesia' (*The migrant*), his life and works allows an entry into the everyday cultural life of this community. Bidesia theatre drew huge audiences, especially when performed by Thakur himself and his acting troupe. The popularity of the plays was due to their narrating common events and experiences related to the pain of migration, a theme that touched a common chord in the hearts of the Bhojpuri audience. The interspersion of comic relief and satire on the existing system also established Bidesia theatre as an extremely popular form of folk art and culture. These plays were also a statement on the existing social dichotomies and the process of displacement of the Bhojpuri migrants.

Thakur gave more of a descriptive picture of society, Pandey's works were seen as more forceful, constantly referring to the overthrow of structures of dominance. A poet who had died in Delhi's Jawaharlal Nehru University in 1989, Pandey had various left wing publications, ranging between issues of repression and resistance. Pandey's work have been highlighted specifically in the context of Dalit and women's movements, as urging its audience to throw away the old order and replace it with a new one. Interestingly, today, the popularity of Pandey's work falls more in the realm of music by bands such as Indian Ocean and films such as Hazaron Khwahishen Aisi (*Thousand desires such as these...*} that have been seen as possessing an aesthetic appeal due to their simple yet powerful tunes that critique dominant bourgeois ideas.

An analysis of both Pandey's and Thakur's work bring out the way in which literature can remain within the realm of aestheticism and propaganda, in spite advocating ideas of change and resistance. In fact, the theme of resistance itself becomes the aesthetic and propagandist enterprise. Thorstein Veblen (1998) had argued that perceptions of beauty are affected by considerations of status, invidious distinction, and pecuniary value. However, if we understand aesthetics as having essentially to do with the sensuous or sensory aspects of experiences, Roland Barthes (1975) in writing about the relation between pleasure and literature, found the experience of aestheticism of the text as unmoored from its ideological and historical context. For him aesthetic experience was basic, and all other things (aesthetic properties, political consciousness, ideologies, false consciousnesses) as secondary in their importance to aesthetic experiences. That is to say, aesthetic experiences, must be explored without pre-conceptions, prejudices, or limitations of either the base or the superstructure. And, truly enough, the vast majority of aesthetic experiences are not focused exclusively, in terms of their contents, on formal or simple-sensory matters. Aesthetic experiences are, first, experiences, and this is a way in which, in the first instance we can locate the works of both Thakur and Pandey.

Moreover, it is also possible to see the manner in which the works of :'hese authors fall within the realm of a kind of literature which is saturated with propagandist practices. This relationship of art, especially, literature to propaganda, in this study has been placed vis-a-vis these writings because Pandey and Thakur's works have been often understood as radical, resistant and carrying the potential to change mentalities and thereby, societies. I argue that these radical writings, rather than reflecting a process of change or challenging the dominant values, end up propagandising the issues at hand. Moreover, these writings not only fall within the realm of propagandist .iterature but gain popularity primarily because they carry an aesthetic appeal.

In the light of the above arguments, the following chapter delves into the various Marxist theories of literature, ranging from those which have seen .iterature as reflecting ideas of the dominant classes, as guided by economic development, changes in the modes of production and exchange, by the consequent division of society into distinct classes and by the struggle of these classes against each other - to those which have held a broader outlook and have acknowledged the presence of other processes and structures (aesthetics and rropagandists) to explain the relationship between literature and society.

CHAPTER 1

Understanding 'Literature' in Marxian Theory

This study begins with a review of the Marxian theories that have addressed the relationship between literature and society. As mentioned, some of these conceptions have argued for a complex interaction between literature and social life, critiquing the value-neutrality and apolitical stances of understanding the generation of a text. While others have shown how literature, although always politically engaged, deals with the prevalent social and political oppressions and may also become a source of aesthetic enterprise. Accordingly, in this chapter we review the work of those scholars who have looked at literature either as a political enterprise, reflecting the dominant values and ideas of a society or of those authors who have although acknowledged the political undertones of literature and its resistance potential, but also view it as an aesthetic endeavour.

Out of those who have addressed the above questions, this study takes account of the writing of Marx and Engels(iQ38, 1970, 1979), Terry Eagleton 1976), Georg Lukacs (1972), Louis Althusser (1977), Lucien Goldmann '97")\ Antonio Gramsci (1977), Pierre Bourdieu (1993 and 1996), Pierre Macherey (1966 and 1995), Alok Rai (2000), K. Updhyaya (1972), Om Prakash Valmiki (2003). Through this debate we see that, the priorities of these different authors of Marxist literary theory are starkly and fundamentally different. Usually these distinctions are based upon how they understand a text, a genre or even the intentionality of the writer.

Literature as reflecting false consciousness:

Marx and Engels

In talking about the reflective nature of literature, Marx and Engels have responded to the social conditions stemming from the rise of capitalism and their theories are therefore formulated specifically to analyze how society functions in a state of upheaval and constant change. The comments of Marx and Engels' on art and literature are scattered and fragmentary. While other art forms find a scarce mention in their work, their analysis of literature (including the text of 'dramas) have significantly shaped and dominated their ideas about aesthetics and culture in general.

Marx's theory of literature is based upon what he termed as, *historical materialism*, a view that explains the course of society as guided by economic development, changes in the modes of production and exchange, by the consequent division of society into distinct and antagonistic classes and by the struggle of these classes against each other. Marx proposed a model of history in which economic and political conditions determine social conditions.

According to Eagleton, Marxist criticism analyses literature in terms of the historical conditions, which produce it. For Eagleton,

Marxist criticism is part of a larger body of theoretical analysis which aims to understand *ideologies*' the ideas, values and feelings by which women and men experience their societies at various times. Moreover, some of those ideas, values and feelings are available to us only in literature. To understand ideologies is thus to understand both the past and the present more deeply. This is one of the reasons why Marxist criticism involves more than what has been set out by the founders of Marxism.

Eagleton says that Marxist criticism is not merely 'Sociology of Literature', concerned with how novels get published and whether they mention the working class. Its aim is to explain[8] the literary work more fully

---

8.   Much non- Marxist criticism would reject a term like 'explanation', feeling that it violates the "mystery' of literature. Eagleton uses

which means a sensitive attention to its forms, styles and meanings (Eagleton, 1976, p 3). Accordingly, within the Marxist frame of thought, literature like all other trends and developments in the modern world can be understood not merely as cultural or ideological, but also strongly social and political. Marxist literary theory has thus emphasized the political in literature.

Within Marx's account of history is the idea that a given individual's social being is determined by larger political and economic forces. Marx writes that 'it is not the consciousness of women and men that determines their being, but, on the contrary, their social being that determines consciousness' (Ibid).

In the same nerve, Marx puts forward his concepts of the base and superstructure. The base is the economic system on which the superstructure rests; cultural activities—such as philosophy or literature-belong to the superstructure. The clear implication of what the 'base' and 'superstructure' is found in the Preface to A

---

it here because he agrees with Pierre Macherey who in his A Theory of Literary Production (Paris, 1966), argues that the task of the critic is not to 'interpret' but to explain'. For Macherey, 'interpretation' of a text means revising or correcting it in accordance with some ideal norm of what it should be; it consists, that is to say, in refusing the text as it is. Interpretative criticism merely changes the meaning of the text for easier consumption. In saying more about the work it succeeds saying less.

Contribution to the Critique of Political Economy (Marx and Engels, 1859): 'In the social production of their life, people enter into definite relations that are indispensable and independent of their will, *relations of production* which correspond to a definite stage of development of their material productive *forces*. The sum total of these relations of production constitutes the economic structure of society, the real foundation, on which raises the legal and political superstructure and to which correspond definite forms of social consciousness. The mode of production of material life conditions the social, political and intellectual life process in general. It is not the consciousness of women and men that determines their being, but on the contrary, their social being that determines their consciousness.'

Art then becomes the part of the superstructure of the society and to understand literature then means understanding the total social process of which it is a part. As the Russian Marxist critic Gregory Plekhanov put it, 'the social mentality of an age is conditioned by that age's social relations (Henri Arvon's *Marxist Aesthetics*, Cornell, 1970). Marx believes that because the base determines the superstructure, it inevitably supports the ideologies of the base. Ideologies are the changing ideas, values, and feelings through which individuals experience their societies. They present the dominant ideas and values as the beliefs of society as a whole, thus preventing individuals from seeing how society actually functions.

The problems of the relationship between art and reality were also addressed by Marxists in a fundamentally new way, on the basis of materialist dialectics. Idealist aesthetics considered art as a reproduction of the ideal, standing over and above actual reality. Marxists consider it absolutely impossible to understand art and literature proceedings only from their internal laws of development. In their opinion, the essence, origin, development and social role of art can only be understood through analysis of the social system as a whole, within which the economic factor -the development of productive forces in complex interaction with production relations - plays the decisive role.

Thus, art as defined by Marxists is one of the forms of social consciousness and it therefore follows that the reasons for its changes should be sought in the social existence of women and men. Marxists give a social explanation of the origin of the aesthetic sense itself. They argue that a person's artistic abilities, her/his capacity for perceiving the world aesthetically, tor comprehending its beauty and for creating works of art appear as a result of the long development of human society and is a product of a person's labor. In his *Economic and Philosophic Manuscripts of 1844*, Marx pointed to the role of labor in the development of human bing's capacity to perceive and reproduce the beautiful and to form objects also 'in accordance with the laws of beauty' (Marx and Engels, *collected Works*, Vol. 3, Moscow, 1975, p. 277). This idea was later developed by Engels in his work *Dialectics of Nature*, in which he noted that efforts of toil 'have given the human hand the high degree of perfection required to conjure into being the pictures of a Raphael, the statues of a Thorwaldsen, the music of a Paganini' (Quoted in Marx and Engels *On Literature and Art*, pp.128-29).

Georg Lukacs

Since Marx's own writing, there have been theorists such as Lukacs and Althusser who have gradually modified or expanded on Marx's original concepts. Lukacs had argued that only realistic forms of fiction are artistically and politically valid. Lukacs, who was writing within the realm of Soviet Socialism, had looked at how 'the commitment of the writer in the forefront emphasized her/his role in the making of a just and equitable environment' (Lukacs, 1972). His essay *'Critical Realism and Socialist Realism'* (1972) is a good example of a polemic held within socialism. This polemic is between critical realism and socialist realism as literary principles on the one hand and between the theory of socialist realism and its practice on the other. Lukacs said that the perspective of critical realism renders great help to the writer to understand the present but it would not enable the writer to conceive the future from inside. This was Lukacs' emphasis. For him, critical realism was thus an objective as for any writer the present offers the entry point into history. This becomes the guiding force which empowers the writer to interpret her/his own reality. On the other hand, the writer of socialist realism is a natural insider and thus no entry point is needed for him because she/he is a participant in the making of a different future.

Lukacs' essay gives an indication as to why the tradition of critical realism gradually weakened in the latter half of the 19th century when writers found it difficult to pursue realism, and when they had to draw on all their inner resources to do justice to their job as writers and as significant voices of their time. This was in the background of the bourgeois-capitalist class becoming reactionary. This situation led to the emergence of socialist realism, which stressed on classlessness as a precondition for real, genuine equality in society.

The problem of sociology of the novel has always preoccupied the sociologists of literature. The novel is also considered as a biography and a social chronicle and thus it can be said here that the social chronicle reflects to a greater or lesser degree the society of the period. The emphasis in the novel is not on the explanation of but on the problem. There is a clear relationship between the literary plane and the everyday life in the society created by liberal economic principles and market production. Lukacs makes this point and says that there is a homology between everyday relations of man and commodities. This relationship extends between some and other people in a market society. Charles Dickens' second novel, *Oliver Twist* (1838), can be considered as an example of a social novel. Social novels centre around the effects of social and economic conditions on the individual, and often aim to bring societal attention to social problems. Such pieces of literature clearly reveal the relationship between the literary plane and the everyday life in the society created by liberal economic principles and market production. Accordingly, it is now possible to move on to a review of literature that delves upon this possibility of art as escaping the premises of dominant ideas.

Literature as breaking away from false consciousness:

Lucien Goldmann

Goldmann in his work '*Towards a Sociology of the Novel*' takes off from Lukacs. Goldmann's hypothesis is concerned with the homology between the structure of the classical novel and the structure of exchange in the liberal economy. Since the exchange in liberal economy is based on the principles of free market capitalist economic system, any work of literature has a possibility to reflect the values of the same economic system. On the other hand, there is also the possibility of the novel to not represent the hegemonic values. Goldmann presents a means to go beyond the actual fictional descriptions of sociological phenomena in order to connect the structure of the literary work itself, not the writer or the consumer, but to the external world. Goldmann's perspective seeks to elucidate structures within a work that may be explained in terms of homologies between these structures and the collective mental structures or categories that shape the consciousness of social groups during a specific time, as well as shaping the imaginary world created by a writer.

One implication of Goldmann's approach is that a writer's work expresses the non-conscious values and aspirations of a collective category, thus the internal structural analysis reveals expressions that are beyond the author's conscious intent. Griswold (1987a) recently expanded Goldmann's scheme to provide a more complete explanation of cultural objects that includes aspects of the writer's intentions and of the work's reception as well as additional cultural circumstances.

Antonio Gramnsci

The Italian theorist Gramsci, with his concept of hegemony, allows for an even more flexible reading of the base/superstructure model. Gramsci believes that ideology alone cannot explain the extent to which people are willing to accept dominant values. He also realizes, along with many other Marxist critics that the base/superstructure model is much too rigid to account for cultural productions, which do not simply reinforce those dominant values.

In a way, Gramsci's notion of hegemony is a continuation of the concepts behind ideology. Hegemony is a sort of deception in which the individual forgets her own desires and accepts dominant values as their own. For example, someone might think that going to college is the right and necessary step in every life, when in reality this belief is socially constructed. This is again one of the several views on the social construction of reality. Thus, on the basis of the above argument, it becomes difficult to generalize how different people engage themselves in making different meanings. Literature, then, may be seen as something that both reinforces dominant values and occasionally calls them into question. For example, nineteenth century women writers of sentimental fiction used certain narrative conventions merely to reinforce dominant values, whereas a writer like Jane Austen used many of the same conventions to undermine the same dominant values.

Louis Althusser

This French Marxist theorist provides a finer understanding of the relationship between literature and ideology. According to Althusser, art cannot be reduced to ideology. Rather, art has a certain *relationship* to ideology. Ideology signifies the imaginary ways in which human beings experience the real world. Literature too gives us this kind of an experience. However, art does more than just passively reflecting the experience. Thus, while Art is held within ideology, it also manages to distance itself from it. This distancing is done to the point where, art permits us to 'feel' and 'perceive' the ideology from which it springs. The difference between science and art is that science gives us conceptual knowledge of a situation; art gives us the experience of that situation, which is equivalent to ideology. By doing this, art allows us to 'see' the nature of that ideology and in the process, moves us towards that full understanding of ideology which is scientific knowledge. (Althusser, L. 1977)

Pierre Macherey

Macherey in his *Theory of Literary Production* (1966 distinguishes between what he calls 'illusion' (meaning false consciousness) and 'fiction'. Illusion is the material on which the writer goes to work. While working on it, the writer lends it a certain shape and structure thereby transforming it into something different. It is by giving ideology a determinate form, fixing it within certain fictional limits, that art is able to distance itself from it, thus revealing to us the limits of that ideology. In doing so, according to Macherey, art contributes to our 'deliverance from the ideological illusion'.

Contending the traditional hermeneutic approach, which perceives literature to be a site of 'essential revelation' and which therefore assumes philosophy to be the unthought-of or not yet thought element in literature, Macherey, in his *Object of Literature* (1995) instead perceives literature to carry within itself the seed of philosophy. Literature thus according to Macherey is not simple primal truth. He tries to express in this book literature's speculative vocation by arguing that literature 'has an authentic value as an intellectual experience...' Here he explains this further by talking about a 'literary philosophy' (1995: 5).

What one can establish out of this is the plain fact that there is no pure discourse. The attempt to delineate philosophy from Literature is an artificial one contextualized in a particular era of History which launched the two as two autonomous paradigms, 'Modern paradigms' as Macherey says (1995:5). The difference between literature and Philosophy thus being 'documentary' (1995:6) in nature, Macherey urges the reader to not ignore or overlook the speculative, the thought, the insight, the foresight, the premonition, the intuition and the mass of knowledge deeply inherent within any literary work. The literary works do not thus merely produce or reproduce a narrative of the society or a description of events. A closer look, a deeper plunge will show that literature actually provides a support to an 'ideological communication' (Macherey, 1995).

Pierre Bourdieu

Pierre Bourdieu's (In *The Field of Cultural Production: Essays on Art and Literature*, Boudieu, P. 1993. Polity Press, Cambridge) analytical method represents a useful alternative to many other eminent modes of analysis ranging from *formalism* to *structuralism* and *deconstruction*, which have dominated literary studies.

Bourdieu dissects the relationship between systems of thought, social institutions and different forms of material and symbolic power. By emphasizing on the structure of power of different kinds, he says that the literature, art and their respective producers do not exist independently of a complex institutional framework which authorizes, enables, empowers and legitimizes them. He has focused on the framework of the structure of power and says that this must be incorporated into any analysis of cultural practices (Bourdieu, 1993).

Bourdieu locates the literary field in the field of power. Similarly, the Bhojpuri literary field[9] can also be analyzed on the same principal and its encounters with the internal social structure i.e. caste system, patriarchy and feudalism, which constitute the field of power in this context. This particular aspect would be dealt in detail in the later part of this chapter and in the subsequent chapter. This book also takes issue with 'reflection theories', with supposed homologies between the structure of work and the social structure or between the works and the worldview of social interests of a specific class. To suggest, in the manner of Lukacs and Goldmann, a writer is somehow an unconscious spokesperson, for a group is for Bourdieu, simply to invert the romantic myth of the poet. Reducing the power to a sort of 'medium', this approach assumes a perfect correlation between the group and the mode of expression without questioning how one defines the group whose world view is supposedly expressed through the work structure (Bourdieu, 1993, p. 13).

According to Bourdieu, by conceiving of literary works as expressions not of the author but rather of the social class of which she or he is a member, by seeing the author as merely one who lends coherence to the structure of her/his class and by positing works as collective products of social groups, such approaches also ignore

---

9.   Literature of Thakur and Pandey in particular.

the objective conditions of the production, circulation and consumption of symbolic goods. They thus fall prey to the objectivism which Bourdieu finds unacceptable in structural analysis. Artistic works in Bourdieu's view are produced by agents existing in objective sets of social relations, which are not limited to those of 'class' and which fulfill specific functions for those agents which must be brought into the analysis.

Reflection theories, no matter how elaborate often neglect the relative autonomy of the literary field. This problem is addressed by for example Mikhail Bakhtin, who suggests that literature is part of, and cannot be understood outside of the 'total context' of a given period's culture. Social and economic factors clearly affect literature but only through their effect on culture as a whole. Their impact on literature per se, occurs only through the mediation of the entire culture (Bakhtin,M. Speech, Genres and other late Essays. Austin: University of Texas Press, 1984, p.2). To counter what he calls the 'short-circuit effect' of approach that posit a direct connection between art and social structure, Bourdieu developed the theory of the field as a social universe with its own laws of functioning (Bourdieu, 1993).

Finally, Bourdieu criticizes the failure of external analysis to consider works of art as possessing a specific language. This does not mean that he accepts the formalist contention that literary language alone can provide an adequate explanation of literature or literary practices. To summerise briefly, Bourdieu's method attempts to incorporate three levels of social reality: the position of the literary or the artistic filed within what he calls the *field of power* (i.e. the set of dominant power relations in society or, in other words, the ruling classes); (2) the structure of the literary field (i.e. the structure of the objective positions occupied by agents competing for legitimacy in the field as well as the objective characteristics of the agents themselves); and (3) the genesis of the producers' habitus (i.e. the structured and structuring dispositions which generate practices) (Bourdieu 1993).

Bourdieu's method can thus be used to analyze the literary field of Bhojpuri. He says that a number of practices and representations of artists and writers can only be explained with reference to the field of power, inside which the literary field is itself in a dominated position. The field of power is the space of relations of force between agents or between institutions having in common the possession of the capital necessary to occupy the dominant positions in different fields, mainly economic or cultural.

It is the site of struggles between holders of different powers or kinds of capital, like the individuals and the class. In the literature of Thakur and Pandey, the confrontation takes place between the state, the landlords, the feudal lords and the deprived masses, masses that are deprived of land, work and other livelihood opportunities and are subject to exploitation by the upper castes.

In the context of languages, a similar contradiction takes place between Hindi and Bhojpuri. What Bourdieu calls the 'economic value', was definitely higher for the Hindi language. This is evident through the scenario of the year 1900, when, 'Sir Anthony MacDonnell, Lieutenant Governor of the North West provinces and Oudh, initiated a move to allow Devanagri to be used in the courts, inaugurating a long conflict over language and script. This move was presaged by a longer history of colonial interventions that sought to distinguish between a Hindu Hindustani and an Urdu Hindustani' (Rai, 2000, pVIII). From this, we can discern the manner in which regional dialects such as Bhojpuri get merely marginalized in the broader context of a literary field (Singh 1991). While Hindi achieved the status of an official language, Bhojpuri was not awarded any recognition by the state. In spite of such discount by the state, Bhojpuri managed to evolve as an alluring language for the production of literary work. As I have discussed in the subsequent chapter, the work of Bhikhari Thakur (one of the most successful Bhojpuri playwrights and actors in the area or eastern UP and Bihar), stands testimony to the popularity of Bhojpuri as a language of literature and art.

According to Bourdieu, the principle of change in works resides in the field of cultural production. Any piece of literature or art either functions as one perpetuating the current conventions, i.e. maintaining the status-quo, or one subverting them and transforming the structure and also the structure of distribution of capital, power, etc. (Bourdieu,1996)

To understand the politics of any language or dialect, there is a need to look at its history. To quote Rai, 'Historically speaking, Hindi has been understood, defined and projected through a series of antithesis: with Urdu; with its 'dialects', notably, *Bray*, with 'provincial' languages; with English. It is sufficient to remark that, in all these antitheses, with their countless local eruptions, there is a curious eruption of innocence and inviolability on the part of Hindi and its protagonists' (Rai, 2005, p. 5). However it can also be mentioned that the popularity of Hindi is not an outcome of government efforts but of the love of the people enshrined in institutions such as Bollywood. The point that I want to draw from Rai's argument is that Hindi, as an official language of the state has dominated its dialects, in particular, Bhojpuri. Bhojpuri is still not scheduled in the 14th *schedule, Constitution of India.*

If one goes into the history of languages, Bhojpuri is an older language than Hindi. The Bhojpuri language has a tremendous amount of writings at its disposal (Upadhyay, 1972).

In contextualising these works within this thesis, I can also clearly locate Macherey's stand in the position I take to show that indeed literature has a bearing on Social Movements. Literature in fact, is in itself a silent revolution. For example, one can mention Om Prakash Valmiki's 'Joothan'-An Untouchable's Life (2003), where the author asserts the identity of a Dalit and gives an account of the hardships faced in the post independent Indian society. Although untouchability was legally abolished in the constitution of the newly independent India in 1949, Dalits continued to face discrimination, economic deprivation, violence, and ridicule. Traditionally, Indian literatures have either ignored untouchables or portrayed them as victims in need of saviors, as objects without voice or agency. Valmiki, through his autobiographical work, has presented an authentic recording of these unrepresented experiences and in the process given voice to the voiceless. He tells the stories of life in the untouchable caste of Chuhra, at the bottom rung of society; his laudable struggle to survive this doomed life of perpetual physical and mental prejudice and intolerance; the obstacles he overcame to become the first high school graduate of his neighborhood; his coming to consciousness under the influence of the great Dalit political leader B. R. Ambedkar; and his transformation into a speaking subject bearing witness to the oppression and exploitation that he endured as an individual and as a member of a stigmatized and subjugated community.

'Dalits today constitute about one sixth of India's population. Spread over the entire country, speaking many languages, and belonging to many religions, they have become a major political force. As a document of the long silenced and long denied sufferings of the Dalits, *Joothan* is not only a contribution to the archives of Dalit history, but a manifesto for the revolutionary transformation of society and human consciousness'(Mukherjee, 2003). The potential of political consciousness that Valmiki demonstrates through his piece of literature needs to be qualified by more sociological investigation. However, there is no denying the important contribution he makes to the Dalit cause by highlighting their problems and miseries. Valmiki, I feel is speaking with in the ambit of ideology as an amalgamation of ideas in accordance to the particular context.

Concluding Remarks

In the contemporary context, Marxist literary criticism has been forced to re-examine its standpoints to evolve an adequate method to cope with these developments. Whereas between the wars, it was the capitalist camp striving to counter the people- oriented socialist thrust in literature. Under such circumstances, Marxist literary theory has turned towards examining a work of art in its specificity. The effort has mainly crystallized as investigation in the forms of literature hitherto, discussion on form, revolved around the idea of human creativity finding new ways to express itself in specific periods of history- epic in ancient times, dramas in periods of transformation from one epoch to another, novel when much later in the 18th century a new powerful social class met the challenge of earning legitimacy and consolidation. This was too broad a perspective. The difficulty particularly was that it interpreted forms in Literature in generic terms- epic, drama, novel etc. as separate kinds of writing in different epochs. It appears necessary now to study the cultural processes in which a particular kind of creative approach takes shape (Ibid).

In this way, we see that the dominant Marxist theories do not always see literature as something dependent solely on hegemonic values and ideas. There are moments where one can find a treatment of literature which is not reducible to merely ideologies or false consciousness. We see that these authors have shown how literature is always politically engaged, to the extent that social and political oppressions themselves become a source of aesthetic enterprise. According to Eagleton (1976), the relationship, which both Althusser and Macherey propose between ideology and literature, is 'deeply suggestive' (p 19). Ideology for both Althusser and Macherey has a certain structural coherence in any society. It is not a mere body of free-floating images. Thus, because it possesses relative coherence, ideology can be the object of scientific analysis; and since literary texts 'belong' to the domain of ideology, they too can become the object of such scientific analysis. A scientific criticism would seek to explain the literary work in terms of the ideological structure of which it is part, yet which it transforms in its art: it would search out the principle which both, ties the work to ideology and distances it from it.

As Engels himself pointed out:

Literature may be a part of the superstructure, but it is not merely the reflection of the economic base. According to F.Engels, "the materialist conception of history, the determining element in history is *ultimately* the production and reproduction in real life. More than this neither Marx nor I have ever asserted. If therefore somebody twists this into the statement that the economic element is the only determining one, she/he transforms it into a meaningless, abstract and absurd phrase. The economic situation is the basis, but the various elements of the superstructure-political forms of the class struggles and its consequences, constitutions established by the victorious class after a successful battle, etc - forms of law- and then even the reflexes of all these actual struggles in the brains of the combatants:

political, legal, and philosophical theories, religious ideas and their further development into systems of dogma- also exercise their influence upon the course of the historical struggles and in many cases preponderate in determining their form" (Eagleton, 1976, p 9).

If we try to uncover the relationship between literature and false consciousness we usually find that there are two possible positions. The first one is that literature reflects a certain kind of false consciousness, which is generally the ideology of the dominant or the dominant ideology. On the other hand we also find a different kind of literature, which reflects certain expressions of the false consciousness, which is against the dominant ideology and in a sense challenges the dominant ideology. The Marxist view based on the Conflict Model, would perceive this literature as reflections of the dominant ideology. Accordingly, in analysing the works of Gorakh Pandey and Bhikhari Thakur, Marxist literary critique forms the basis as it seeks to assess the political tendency of a literary work and yet shows how art can transcend the ideological limits of its time, yielding us insight into the realities which ideology hides from view.

The theoretical background for the debates useful for my argument has thus been laid out in this chapter. One will now explore the role of select Bhojpuri literature and the debates around the same, in the Indian context in general and Eastern UP and Bihar in particular. More specifically, one undertakes to look at the Bhojpuri writings of Pandey and Thakur and their implications on the Bhojpuri society. This will allow me to analyze the link between literature and society. In the light of the review of different approaches in the sociology of literature and art, one tries to examine the following questions, with specific reference to select Bhojpuri Literature.

a. What are the main social themes reflected in such Bhojpuri Literature?

b. What kind of analysis and action is advocated by such literature?

c. To what extent is this literature a social product?

d. In what ways do these works serve as propaganda for the status quo; or does it try to undermine it?

CHAPTER 2

An Analysis of Bhikhari Thakur's Work

It is said that in Bhikhari Thakur's (1887-1971) work, there is a specific style of subtle protest against the oppressive and corrupt system, which raises some questions in the viewer's minds, leaving them at liberty to be ashamed, silenced, shocked or to rise in protest against the social ills depicted in the plays. In this section, there is an argument that the socio-political realities depicted in Thakur's work gain popularity not merely because they depict social ills inflicted upon the marginalized sections of society (especially women and Dalits) and are thus resistant towards the dominant norms but because his work resorts to the propagandist and entertainment spheres. They undertake a political motive but fall in the realm of cultural pleasure. Thakur, by making use of the Bidesia folk songs, folklore, proverbs and popular sayings of the Bhojpur belt successfully achieved this popularity. These became a good medium not only to create awareness but also create the cultural definition of this region.

Indeed, it is possible to analyse the essence of aesthetics in the literature and art in also through regional dialect of Bhojpuri used by Thakur. This can be analyzed in the changing social, political and economic scenario such that although the significance of local dialects like Bhojpuri have been undermined vis a vis Hindi as a language and literature, the role of Bhojpuri and other local dialects have been essential in establishing Hindi itself as a language of literature. This presupposes a modification in the relationship between the circulation of language and the social distribution of several ideas. If the techniques of artistic modernity have reshaped the way art relates to the everyday, they have also lent themselves to a whole apparatus of intellectual elitism that serves to reinforce the existing 'social distribution of ideas'. For exactly this reason, Bourdieu had coined the term "cultural capital." As Ranciere himself acknowledges elsewhere, the theater of Brecht, for instance, is formally the same whether it is performed at a union hall or for hoity-toity intellectuals -it's the kind of social forces that make use of something that determine politics, not what "regime" it belongs to.

Local level literature mostly exhibits the society, its civilization and culture. It deals with the everyday life of the common woman and man. Besides, it also reflects the struggle in the everyday life of people for the betterment of their lives (Pandey, 2006). His plays on the issues like widow marriage, migration, child marriage and caste system have entertained the people of the Bhojpur region. Besides, they have also been able to spread an awareness among people through the system of ideas. His play 'Bidesia' gained immense popularity. It is about a migrant person who goes to Calcutta in search of work. The social science institute, Allahabad did a project on Bidesia and remarked, 'Bidesia is a phrase designation about the people who left their country and did not return and the tradition of performing art was rooted in this migration'. The work of Thakur becomes relevant in the light of above mentioned arguments. He has successfully protected the Bhojpuri culture in his plays.

As mentioned, contrary to the arguments forwarded by the Marxian Literary Theory, it is possible to see Thakur's work as moving away from the dominant bourgeois ideologies. They do to a certain extent resist the dominant ideologies. Moreover, this literature reflects ideas about the way in which this society is organized. It reflects the social influences of the authors and the means by which their literary products reach an audience. It tells us how the sociohistorical context (defined by historical time, economic and political structure, social stratification, and cultural orientation) influence the style and content of the authors' works. Furthermore, it is possible to take Thakur's literature as an enterprise of aesthetics, so that it can be analysed and experienced purely in terms of its entertainment or pleasure value. Thakur's writings which have been often understood as resistant and carrying the potential to change mentalities and thereby societies, can also be understood as propagandist. I argue that these radical writings, rather than reflecting a process of change or challenging the dominant values, end up propagandizing the issues at hand.

Indeed, the reviews about the Thakur's work reflect the very manner in which any work can be understood as propagandist.

Bhikhari Thakur is a Bhojpuri public poet in reality. The Bhojpuri people see the aspects of good and bad things about their lives in his plays. He was a brilliant writer on the issues pertaining to rural life.

Dr. Uday Narayan Tiwari ('Bhojpuri Bhasha aur Sahitya' PP.44-45)

Bhikhari Thakur became very famous by writing and presenting plays about people's everyday life. This man alone popularized Bhojpuri more than anybody else. He through his Bhojpuri plays successfully campaigned for the Bhojpuri language in the Bhojpuri speaking area.

Dr. Krishnadev Upadhyay ('Bhojpuri Sahitya ka Itihas, PP.409)

Accordingly, this chapter seeks to analyze some of the literature produced in Eastern Uttar Pradesh and Bihar by Bhikhari Thakur. Thakur's well known works are mainly in the form of plays. He has also written some songs in Bhojpuri. His famous song 'Ae sajni re' from the film 'Hazaaron khwaishein aisi' is a good example (Directed by Sudhir Mishra,2005). The aim of this chapter is to contextualize his works of literature in their social contexts.

Thakur was born in 1887 in a small village in Chapra district of Bihar. Thakur was a barber by caste and came from a very poor family. Thakur was a poet, lyricist, playwright, play director, folk musician and an actor at the same time. He was equally dexterous in all these creative fields. He successfully adopted the features of the traditional form of theatrical presentations but at the same time, did not hesitate in bringing about improvisations when the situation demanded. The themes of Thakur's plays circulated around the pertinent issues of the existing society. The dialogue in his plays is mainly in the form of poetry, but in order to make it more interesting and entertaining, he also used easy colloquial language. He did not design his stage according to the conventional norms. They used be open from three sides and very simple, generally in the form of a raised rectangular platform. One side was closed with the help of a tent sheet. The very important feature of his plays thus turn out be their dialogic nature. This kept people involved and interested.

This was perhaps the first experiment of this kind in any theatrical style in India (Singh, 2005). It refused the norm of theatre as being a building where people entered and positioned in a stratified way to witness the theatre spaces. It reminded constantly that theatre was a public act. A dialectic between traditions and conventions and the challenges of contemporary world gave rise to new experiments and made his theatre dynamic. Moreover, the main tendency exhibited in his plays was social issues raised through entertainment.

Thakur's plays lead us through the many layers of India's rural society, giving an insight into their plight, philosophy towards life and difficult circumstances under whose mounting pressure Thakur became a writer and a theatre person. He belonged to the lower section of the society and given his caste status, this very fact forms the basis from which all his creative writings took off (Upadhyay, 1972). Under such conditions, he managed to do some theatre in his day-to-day activities and thus proved to be defiant enough to launch a drive against the existing circumstances in the society, which was inflicted with feudalism and casteism. The times of Bhikari Thakur were full of political, social, economic turmoil. In the turbulent period of India's struggle for freedom, he took up the cause of the neglected and agonized women of rural India. This proved to be the starting point in his long journey of creative writing. For Thakur, the liberation of India as a country had an equal and parallel meaning in the liberation of the rural women from their miseries. He fought relentlessly for the cause of women abandoned by their husbands in search of a livelihood to bigger cities and towns and the brutal practice of selling young girls to older men on the pretext of marriage (Singh,2005). In spite of underprivileged circumstances, Thakur managed to become a famous playwright (Singh,2005).

Thakur was very influenced by the social movements of Bengal. He minutely analysed the dichotomies persistent in his own society after coming back from Calcutta (present day Kolkata). He decided to problematise the issues around economy, religion, caste and gender based exploitation through folk theatre and folk songs. He wrote many plays around these issues between 1919 to 1965 and with his theatre troupe, travelled and performed them to spread the message of awareness in the Bhojpuri speaking belt. He received a lot of admiration from the poor, discriminated and uneducated Bhojpuri public.

Thakur's work and Bidesia Folk Tradition in Bhojpuri

Bidesia was the affectionate form of address given to the migrants by their loved ones who were left behind in their homeland, and so lent its name to the new folk culture that emerged out of this migration, namely, the *Bidesia* folk culture. This folk culture is represented in many forms such as *nautanki* (musical theatre), drama, folk songs and folk paintings. During this migration period, a form of folk theatre, also called *Bidesia* emerged in the Bhojpuri region. Bidesia theatre drew huge audiences especially when performed by Bhikhari Thakur and his acting troupe. Thakur composed many popular bidesia plays which were filled with songs based on folk tunes such as *lorikayan, jantsari, sorthi, birha, barahmasa, chaupayi etc.* Thakur's first play known as *Bidesia*, is one of the most famous plays in Eastern UP and Bihar. Bhikhari's immense popularity in this region makes him a minor legend. (Bhikhari Thakur Rachnavali, 2005). There are hundreds of natak companies in Eastern UP and Bihar who call themselves as 'Bidesia style natak companies' and they are very popular in the area (Upadhyay, 1972). Thakur's play *Bidesia* brought him instant fame and popularity. His other play *Beti Bechwa* is about the plight of young girls married to older men. The feudal set up is not amused by his activities and notices the impact of his populariy. That is how Bhikhari Thakur becomes a legend in his own life time (Sulabh, 2006).

The popularity of all his plays was due to the narration of common events and experiences, related to the pain of migration, a theme that touched a common chord in the Bhojpuri audience. The combination of comic relief and satire on the existing system also established Bidesia theatre as an extremely popular form of folk art and culture. These plays were also a statement on the existing social dichotomies like exploitation based on class, caste, gender and process of displacements of the Bhojpuri migrants (Tiwari, 2005).

The Literature of Bhikhari Thakur: Gender

Thakur, through his plays analysed the lives of women, their social condition and psychology in the existing rural setting. He attempted to elucidate many aspects of women's lives for instance, by looking at the life of a young girl in the plays *Beti Viyog* (The separated daughter) and *Nand Bhojai*. He looked at the lives of married women, in his plays, *Bhai Virodh*, *Ganga Snan*, *Putra Vadh*, and women with migrant husbands in the plays *Bidesia*, *Vidhwa Vilap*, *Gabar Ghichor* and *Kalyug Prem*. In these latter plays, Thakur shows how the women take care of the household and livelihood of the children. The heroine of the play *Kalyug Prem* takes care of the family and bears the hardships as her husband is an alcoholic. Thakur also addresses the issues of chastity of women left behind by their husbands during migration. The problem of dowry and the exploitation of women by men is clearly depicted in the play *Beti Viyog* where the greedy father sells his daughter *Akhjo* to a rich old man who dies soon after the marriage, while *Akhjo* spends the rest of her life as a widow. In the play *Vidhwa Vilap*, the same *Akhjo* has to face physical exploitation and economic miseries at the hands of her affinal kin.

In the play *Gabar Gichor*, Thakur created a very radical character of a woman whose migrant husband does not return for fifteen years. In between she develops a physical relation with another man and gives birth to a child. Despite a lot of accusations and exploitation, she successfully fights and takes care of her child. Thakur, in this play seems to be fighting for the freedom of women and the wish to bring up their children.

As mentioned before, this is not to say that Thakur did not conform to the understood norms of the society. Through his plays he glorified the status of women as mothers and virtuous daughters-in-law. In the play *Ganga Snan*, he is very critical about the character of the daughter-in-law and almost portrays her as a disrespectful woman, keeping in mind her behaviour towards her mother-in-law. In the play *Putra Vadh*, he focused on the affection of *Badki* (name of the mother) towards her son *Chetram*. In the play *Bidesia*, he talked about the problem of prostitution as a social problem and also suggested ways for the rehabilitation of sex workers.

The Literature of Bhikhari Thakur: Dalits and the Caste system

Thakur was himself born in a backward caste family of barbers. In the existing feudal society, barbers, apart from their caste services had to render their duties in all the rituals of the upper caste. They were very much part of the *Jajmani System* and depended economically and socially upon their patrons (higher castes). They were often paid in kind for their services according to the laws of the *Jajmani System*. Apart from this, they were subject to exploitation by the feudal lords and the dominants of the village quite often. Thakur himself had experienced all these hardships. So it was the same *Nai* (Barber), uneducated and classified society that he had in mind when he wrote his plays. The subject matter of his plays therefore showed the day-to-day challenges of this class. Perhaps, the most important aim of his plays was to create an awareness about these contradictions in the lives of the underclass and also suggest ways to get rid of these miseries.

The key issues that he dealt with were child-marriage, uneven marriages (young girl married to an old man), selling off daughters for wealth, families getting nuclear in a lust of wealth and property, crime, addiction, theft, gambling etc. The result of these plays was felt very soon and selling of daughters for wealth was criticised and looked down upon by everyone. Widow remarriage was promoted and incidentally, during the same period, child marriage was banned by the government (Singh,2005).

The names of the characters in his plays also came from the Dalit and other lower caste communities, e.g. *Updar Udwas, Jhatul, Chitru* etc. as during this time, Dalits and other lower castes usually did not have names like other upper caste names. The other important fact here is that, most of his actors belonged to the lower castes. Therefore, it can be said here that, Thakur took all encouraging steps through his work and made every affirmative endeavor for the development and appraisal of the Dalit and lower caste communities (Tiwari, 2005).

Bhikhari Thakur through his work reflects the system of various ideas on which the contemporary society was organized. Sometimes he conforms to the societal values and norms of the feudal, patriarchal society, especially in his plays Bidesia and Kalyug Prem, where he argues that a woman should be chaste to her husband and take care of the family, household and children. Thus Thakur also keeps falling back to the same kind of false consciousness that he constantly tried to break away from.

Although, it is clear that Thakur in his plays is propagandizing for women's promiscuity. But at the same time he also fights for the freedom of women and their sexual rights in the play *Gabarghichor*. The positive aspect of the play *Bidesia*, at the same time is that, in this play he talks about prostitution as a social problem. If we bring in the base and superstructure model here, then we can see that this kind of work is a result of the economic base. Since Bhikhari came from a backward caste family, he was too poor to lead his life in a normal way. The social and economic circumstances compeled him to migrate and earn his living (Singh, 2005). So, he had lived through all these miseries and exploitation caused by the dominant classes and produced a work, which in a way, are viewed against the contemporary social practices. Since all his plays directly talk about the dalits and the underclass. His theatre troop was also mainly comprised of dalits and lower caste people (Bhikhari Thakur Rachnavali). The names of the characters in his plays are also dalit and lower caste names. According to Macherey, literature gives support to ideological communications. Bhikhari's works, along the same line, has definitely provided some kind of ideological communication. The selling of daughters for wealth was considered to be a matter of low prestige and a misdeed, prohibited child marriages during the same period (Singh, 2005). The subject matter of Thakur's work was influenced by the social practices and he wanted others to become aware of their miseries. He wanted to propagate a kind of consciousness among people through his writings which comes close to what Luckacs meant when he talked about socialist realism as a perfect form of creativity, where the writer gets first hand information, lives it, and produces authentic arguments.

As we'll see in the next chapter, both Thakur and Pandey's work reflect this similar mode of practice that is of combining the political with the aesthetical. As Ranciere argues, both politics and aesthetics are concerned with imagining, envisioning, and even creating, yet aren't the kinds of things these fields of inquiry imagine, envision and create greatly disparate? He argues that what is at stake in politics, just as it is in aesthetics, is the distribution of the sensible, and that politics happens through the disruption of a certain aesthetic organization of sense experience. Based on the above discussion, it can be said that Thakur made an impact in the field of the political through his work but there is no denying the fact that his plays were primarily a form of entertainment. Besides, they contained a system of ideas which some times conformed to the societal values and sometimes deviated from them. In the following chapter, we can locate similar traits in the work of Gorakh Pandey, whose corpus of literature has been seen as more radical than Thakur's.

CHAPTER 3

An Analysis of Gorakh Pandey's Work

In this chapter, I look at the literature produced by the Bhojpuri revolutionary/radical writer, Gorakh Pandey, who has mainly written poems and songs as opposed to the work of playwright Bhikhari Thakur. Surely then, the way in which Pandey's literature relates to the society has a different fascination. Although pertaining to the socio-political realm of the Bhojpur belt, Pandey's work confluences with an aesthetical enterprise, drawing primarily on folk languages. As mentioned in the previous chapter, politics shares certain modalities with the senses. Ranciere points out that politics first becomes a possibility with the institution of a community, whereas a community itself begins with something in common. This commonality is no shared stock of goods or shared claim to a territory. Rather, it is a shared partition of the sensible. Community pivots around common modalities of sense. In other words, the commonality upon which a community is founded is sense, and politics first becomes a possibility with the institution of 'common sense'. Moreover, this distribution of the sensible is an aesthetic enterprise, and what is at stake in any politics is aesthetics.

Drawing this correlation between aesthetics and the distribution of the sensible and, ultimately, between aesthetics and politics now requires a precise understanding of the term. Aesthetics according to Ranciere is not any set of artistic practices nor is it the general theory that concerns these practices. Indeed, aesthetics is not even a theory of sense experience at large. Rather, if the correlation between politics and aesthetics is to be exposed, Ranciere insists aesthetics must be understood in the terms of Kant's Critique of Pure Reason. Aesthetics is 'the system of a priori forms determining what presents itself to sense experience.'

Moreover, the relation aesthetics bears to politics is analogous to the relation Kant's a priori forms bear to sense experience. Just as these a priori forms determine the organization of human experience and provide its conditions, aesthetics comes in various structural systems that serve both to condition the shared world of our daily experience and to partition that world and delimit the positions one might occupy within it. Politics is not reducible to the sensible but can be thus conditioned by aesthetics, just as sense experience is conditioned by the a priori.

It is in this light that we begin to understand Pandey's songs. According to Singh, creativity in the language of literature is based on the folk languages or dialects (Singh, 1991). We find a similar approach in most of Pandey's work which uses folk language and tries to lend it the strength and courage to break through the fabric of conservatism.

To support this argument, one can appreciate Manager Pandey's (1989) assertion that Bhojpuri poetry is primarily the poetry of the people which does not include court poetry in its arena. The poetry of the nineteenth century reflects the awareness of contemporary society in this way: there was a major influence on the Bhojpuri literature by the arrival of railways as a part and parcel of contemporary capitalism, which affected the social relations in a major way. This brought people in a state of conflict with the situation and was expressed in this manner:

> The rail is not the enemy
>
> The ship is not the enemy
>
> The one which took my husband away...
>
> The money is not the enemy

(quoted in Upadhyay, 1972).

Emphasis of opposition in this song is not merely on the imperialist and colonialist mode of production, rather on the ideology and character of mode of production. Imperialism as a system based on profit and loss in monetary terms influences social and human relations in a big way. This becomes the essence of the above song.

Gorakh Pandey: Life and Cultural Personality

Gorakh Pandey was born in 1945 in a village called 'pandit ke munderwa' in Deoria district of Uttar Pradesh. He finished his masters in literature from Sampoornanand Sanskrit University. He was also elected as the President of the student union in the same University. He did another M.A. in Philosophy from Kashi Hindu Vishwavidyalaya (BHU) in 1973. He presented a small research book in the same University. The title of the book was 'dharma ki marxwadi awdharna' (Marxist interpretation of religion). According to the Indian Philosophy, the word *Dharma* has a bigger meaning and it doesn't have any equivalence to the English word *religion*. Although, the common usage of the word finds it's meaning close to the English word *religion*. Pandey dissociated himself from the mainstream Hindi poetry since the Naxalbari movement of 1969. He associated himself with the peasant movements of those times and became an active volunteer in the countryside. He was very active in the Allahabad, Varanasi and Lucknow districts. He motivated a lot of people to join these movements and wrote a lot of poems and songs for the movement during this period. His collection 'Bhojpuri ke nau geet' (nine songs in bhojpuri) was published in 1978. He joined Jawahar Lal Nehru University as a research scholar in philosophy in 1980's. He wrote a book on Sartre. He is Said to have committed suicide diagnosed as caused by schizophrenia on 29 January 1989 in JNU. He was a research associate in Philosophy at that time.

Pandey has mainly written on the issue of inequality, exploitation etc. in the light of the caste system. The same essence can be very vividly visualized in the poem 'Achhut' ki Shikayat' (Complaint of an Untouchable) in the words of Hira Dom, which was published in September 1914 in a magazine called 'Saraswati'[10]. The poem goes like this:

> 'We are being exploited day and night,
>
> We have to beg before our masters.
>
> Even God does not care about our miseries,
>
> How long will this exploitation continue?'

This poem stands as a testimony to the nature of the social condition. This is the story of Hira Dom's exploitation, agony and helplessness. The poem originates straight from the heart of a *Dalit* and thus is different from the poetry which is written in a sympathetic mode towards dalits (Pandey, 2006).

---

[10]   Quoted in singh,2005, p 6.

Poems and songs like the one discussed above are good examples of Bhojpuri literature dealing with the lives of the oppressed masses. The Bhojpuri folksongs like any other revolutionary compositions in any other language depict the weight of social and political changes. This is the reason why there are songs in Bhojpuri on 1857, Gandhi's spinning wheel and on Bhagat Singh etc (Pandey, 2006). Hindi cinema has started using Bhojpuri folksongs.

There have been a number of continuous peasant movements in eastern UP and Bihar before independence and post independence as well. These movements have led to strong political awareness in the lives of people of the area, which is reflected in the Bhojpuri literature (Pandey, 2006). The same trend can be further traced in the songs of Gorakh Pandey. His poems have a very close relationship with the peasant struggles which took place between the period 1972-1979 in the nearby areas of Patna and Bhojpur. Pandey's poetry in Bhojpuri and Hindi was also influenced by the Naxalbari peasant struggle. He has connected them to the ongoing struggle against inequality. The agony of the deprived people in his poems and songs is not momentary but a result of an older ongoing struggle, which is thousands of years old. In his own words:

> 'Their agonies are thousands of years old,
> Their envy is thousands of years old,

> I am only articulating their words and communicating with a rhythm and flow.
>
> But you are scared because you believe I am provoking' (Quoted in Pranaykrishna, 2004, p.22).

Pandey started writing in a phase which was marked by various peasant struggles as discussed above and there was a drive from the state to suppress it and crush the revolution and the revolutionaries. His poems in Bhojpuri are excellent examples of something which is local and at the same time has the flavor of modern scientific and materialistic awareness (Pranay Krishna, 2004).

His poetry is not just about the struggles of the peasants but also questions and provides answers to the complexities of the class struggle, articulation of the peasant's uprisings with the proletarian consciousness, Marxist interpretation of the public services and explanation of the structure of the Indian state, provides a logical interpretation of the experiences of the peasant struggle. Besides, he was very sensitive towards women and has written many poems on their exploitation by the zamindars/landlords.

The zamindars are still there in every village, And they still exploit women in the fields of pulses.

The above poem talks about the manner in which landlords and their men exploited women at their workplaces. This mainly happens with the women working in their fields, that is why, Pandey talks about a 'demon' who lives in the fields of pulses and grains. The mischievous spirit figure is associated with the landlord in the above poem by Gorakh Pandey.

For Pandey, the elegance of folk art and literature and its acceptance are crucial. He says that any piece of literature should be written in such a way that its reader or user or listener should be the masses, the exploited masses themselves (Krishna, 2004). Precisely for the same reason, one of his songs on holi becomes a song of peasant exploitation by the feudal lords:

'Tell me, you accountant to the landlord,

In whose name is this land?

Who does this land belong to?

What book, what pen?

What horse, what reins?

Courts, summons, whose rides? Who does
and who repays? Whose efforts beautify this
earth? And who eats the best of rice? Winter,
summer, rain or slime,

I can no more tell the difference. It is I who husked the wheat,

It is I who turned into husk. We have lost all our values,

We are punished and whenever we say no, The rich man has a feast in his house,

He sets ablaze our house and watches it burn,

And gives us a threatening look when we say anything. One whose entire life was spent amidst the lands, Where has his boat been lost?

We are slaves of those who are, Miles away from this land.

We have shed our sweat and blood, And yet have lost everything.

But now this is the limit of our patience, Now we farmers and labourers shall unite, And take our rights from these thieves.'

-Pandey, Zameen, 1976 (Pranaykrishna, 2004).

The above song talks about the issues of absentee landlordism who stays away from his fields but still rules. The solution of the problem comes in the last four lines of the song where there is an urge to get united and take back their lands from the landlord.

As I have already mentioned, creating a consciousness among the masses is the sole aim of his poems/songs. This can be seen in his other poems such as *Samanti Punjipati Raj Satta ka Charitra* (The character of the feudal and capitalist state), *Kursi Nama*(Biography of the chair), *Unka Dar* (Their Fear), *Swarg se Bidai* (Departure from heaven), *Bhoohhi Chidiya hi Kahani* (Story of a Hungry Bird), *Bhediya* (The Jackal). The other facet of his poetry is communist internationalism", which becomes clear in his very famous song 'Janta ke Paltaniya' (Platoons of the Masses). The aim of this song is to articulate all kinds of movements against all kinds of exploitations and there is a vision of a world which is free and without exploitation of any kind and degree. The song goes like this:

> 'When the platoons of the masses move,
>
> The earth shakes..
>
> Europe, USA, Asia, Africa...
>
> All the four continents shake..'

The meaning is that, the whole world, especially the British Empire, USA, Africa and Asia or one can say that the first and the third world, are all under the influence of the mass movements of different kind, based on their different contexts.[11]

---

11. With the aim to articulate all kind of movements across national boundaries.

In Pandey's poems and songs, we also find a drive against the notion of imperialism and feudalism. Pandey himself was closely associated with the 'Indian People's Front' which was formed in 1982 by the initiative of the Communist Party of India (ML). In 1985, Gorakh Pandey became the pioneer general secretary of the 'Jan Sanskriti Manch'which is the progressive cultural and literary forum of CPI (ML). The reality of the mass struggle against the same is very clear in his literature. The ideology of Marx and Lenin is of course the main philosophy behind his composition. In the above poem he has clearly mentioned their names in a form of a slogan. The four lines on Marx, Lenin and Mao talk about how Marx and Lenin have led the movement by their ideology. Mao provides light to the movement, meaning to say that he shows the path.

In another poem, *Inquilaab ke Geet* (Song of Revolution), Pandey had discussed the various problems that the poor people face and through this song, he explains their agony and provides a solution to their problem. The song goes like this:

> 'The name of our wishes is inquilaab, The
> name of our endeavour is inquilaab,
>
> The only work we have today is inquilaab,
>
> The answer to all the loot and plunder is
> inquilaab, The answer to all the deprivation is
> inquilaab,

> The answer to all our questions is inquilaab,
> End of all feudal powers is inquilaab,
>
> End of all those who dominate is inquilaab,
> Development of every new world is inquilaab,
> Destruction is inquilaab,
>
> Development is inquilaab,
>
> Listen! The voice of the downtrodden is
> inquilaab. Open up because the ray of hope is
> inquilaab,
>
> Stand up because the only way for the
> deprived like us is inquilaab.
>
> Go on, because the call of the time is inquilaab.'

In another poem Pandey deals with the problems of peasants and landless labourers. The title of the poem is *Guhar* (A Request).

In this poem, the fellow peasants motivate each other to stand up for their rights and take back their land from the landlords. The poem goes like this:

The struggle of the farmers has now started, Come fight alongside us oh big brother. How long shall you sleep with your eyes closed? And how long dreams of joy shall you see? Drops of your sweat turn everything to gold, But they suck you dry and fill their tummies. And you are left but with a handful of grain. Come fight with us oh, big brother. They build their armies with your children

And order them to shoot your way. This is not a prison, but a court house they say. Come fight with us oh, big brother. The world is on your finger tips But all you get is the fire of hell. Wake up, we have to overthrow this structure, Come fight with us oh, big brother. This army has been born of your own blood. The red army of farms and factories, Is calling you night and day, Come fight with us oh, big brother.

Concluding Remarks

Pandey himself was a Marxist and a member of the CPI (ML). His songs talk about the exploitation caused by the upper caste landlords and dominant castes on the poor and underclass masses. Some of his poems like *Ab Nahi, Inquilab and Guhaar* talk about the call of revolution against the exploiters. These poems also suggest that now the peasants have identified themselves as a class and there is a feeling for class for itself in them. They are even ready to pick up arms and shed blood. On the other hand, there are poems like *Jameen, Janta Ke Paltaniya and Guhaar*, which give the description of the miseries and helplessness of the underclass caused by the upper castes, State, Police, etc.

Pandey, an intellectual from Jawahar Lal University, New Delhi, comes from a Bhojpuri speaking area and was very active in that area, so he did not need an entry point in the field to react on. This is similar to Bourdieu's literary field which is located in the field of power. The power here was in the hands of upper castes and Pandey's literature is produced as a form of negation to that kind of power and there is a contradiction between the classes; the ruling class and the exploited class. The interesting fact here is that Pandey himself belonged to a Brahmin family which is considered to be an upper class. So, Pandey was powerful in the field of power.

As pointed out by Macherey and Althusser, any piece of literature is guided by some kind of ideology. Literature is a part of ideological structure but there is a possibility that the literature/ art ties with the ideology and also distances itself from it. In the first case, literature reflects a certain kind of ideology, which is generally the ideology of the dominant and in the second case it reflects a kind of ideology, which is against the dominant ideology and in a way challenges the dominant ideology. Pandey's literature here falls in the second category, which also challenges the ideology of the dominant classes and poses a threat against them. It is clearly suggested through his poems and songs. The content of his work mainly describes the social situation of the lower classes in the local social structure. These poems and songs, according to the content, bear a potentiality to propagandize against the status-quo. Pandey's work is a form of propaganda. Prpopagandist art is a genre by itself e.g. 'Mile sur mera Tumhara' which was once broscasted for years by Doordarshan (the state

Television channel) and acclaimed intense popularity and helped in propagandizing the spirit of nationalism.

Eagleton, in his book, *Marxism and Literary Criticism* (1976), says that literature may be a part of the superstructure, but is not merely the reflection of the economic base. Now the argument is that, if this is the case then any piece of literature would reflect a dominant ideology, then how does Pandey's work fit in the Marxist scientific analysis of base and superstructure ? Engels' reply to Joseph Block in 1890 makes it clearer. Engels said that, economic situation is the basis of every kind of production and reproduction in the society. But if the argument is twisted into economic element being the only determining aspect, then it would be a wrong hypothesis. Various elements of superstructure, political forms of class struggles, its consequences, forms of law, religious ideas, and philosophies also determine the form of the ideological structure. So, it can be said here that Pandey's poems and songs are the connecting links in the ongoing struggle against all kinds of exploitation.

The main themes reflected in the analysis of the select literature revolve around the issue of work, right to live with dignity, ownership of land, equality, exploitation of women by the landlords and rural elite, hierarchy based on caste system etc. The nature of action advocated in the songs of Pandey is very radical in nature. He promotes the peasants to overthrow the structure of dominance, take over the land and if necessary take up arms as well.

On the basis of the arguments made above, it can be suggested that this kind of literature is a social product, because it is produced in the society and consumed as well. But at the same time it is very difficult to make overarching statements about literature in general. This body of literature also propagandizes to undermine the status-quo.[12] So, Pandey is also a product and not a free agent of the literary field. On the basis of the above discussions on Pandey's work, it can be said that being an intellectual and an upper caste, he managed to write on the social conditions of his society. His work can be seen close to Lenin's idea of 'ideology' which can contain any system of ideas. I would not say here that his work should be seen here as entertainment but definitely carrying some sets of ideas and specific form of propaganda art.

Thus we see that first there is a process of depoliticization at play in the given social-political formations, that is, it prevents those excluded or marginalized from speaking and thereby assuming the right to speak. Second, the emergence of politics itself, which emerges through the antagonism of a given order, has aesthetics at its core to the extent that it can bring about a redistribution of the sensible, a shift in public consciousness concerning how we see, what is seen.

---

[12]   Pranaykrishna, 2004, P 10-14.

CHAPTER 4

Aesthetics, politics & culture in 'Bidesia' art.

In this chapter, there is an attempt to explore on the elements of aesthetics, politics and culture in Bhojpuri 'Bidesia' art form. Bidesia art form was developed by the famous Bhojpuri 'play write and artist' Bhikhari Thakur in the early 20th century. .

It is believed that bhojpuri 'Bidesia' art form designed by Bhikhari Thakur manifests a specific style of minute protest against the oppressive and deceitful system, which advances some questions in the viewer's minds, leaving them free to feel repentant, silenced, stunned or to get-up in disapproval against the social problems depicted in the plays. In this chapter there is an argument that the socio-political realities portrayed in Bidesia art gain popularity not merely because they depict social ills inflicted upon the marginalized sections of society (especially women and Dalits) and are thus resistant towards the dominant norms but because his art centres to the propagandist and entertainment spheres. They undertake a political motive but fall in the realm of aesthetics and cultural pleasure. Bidesia folk songs, folklore, proverbs and popular sayings of the Bhojpur belt of Bihar successfully achieved this popularity. These became a good medium not only to create awareness but also create the cultural definition of this region as a celebration of the beauty of bhojpuri folk culture which is very well articulated and depicted through 'Bidesia' art form.

Indeed, it is possible to analyse the essence of aesthetics in the literature and art also through regional dialect of Bhojpuri used in Bidesia art.

This can be analysed in the changing social, political and economic scenario such that although the significance of local dialects like Bhojpuri have been undermined vis a vis Hindi as a language and literature, the role of bhojpuri and other local dialects have been essential in establishing Hindi itself as a language of literature. If the techniques of artistic modernity have reshaped the way art relates to the everyday, they have also lent themselves to a whole apparatus of intellectual elitism that serves to reinforce the existing 'social distribution of certain ideas'. For exactly this reason, Bourdieu had coined the term "cultural capital." As Ranciere himself acknowledges elsewhere, the theatre of Brecht, for instance, is formally the same whether it is performed on a political stage or for group of learned people. -it's the kind of social forces that make use of something that determine politics, not what "regime" it belongs to.

Local level literature and art mostly reflects the society, its civilization and culture. It deals with the everyday life of the common women and men. Besides, it also exhibits the struggle in the everyday life of people for the betterment of their lives (Pandey, 2006). Bidesia art covers issues like widow remarriage, migration, child marriage and caste system,that has entertained the people of the Bhojpur region. Apart from this, it has also been able to spread an awarenesss among people through the system of ideas. 'Bidesia' gained immense popularity. Character Bidesia is about a migrant person who goes to Calcutta in search of work. The social science institute, Allahabad did a project on Bidesia and remarked, 'Bidesia is a kind of expression about the people who left their country and did not return and the tradition of performing art was embedded in this migration'. Bidesia art form becomes relevant in the light of above mentioned arguments. Bhojpuri folk culture is successfully protected in Bidesia art.

It is possible to see Bidesia art as getting away from the dominant bourgeois ideologies. Bidesia art to a certain extent confronts the dominant beliefs. Moreover, this

Art form considers ideas about the way in which this society is coordinated. It reflects the social influences on dalits and lower castes and the means by which their cultural products reach an audience. It tells us how the sociohistorical context (defined by historical time, economic and political structure, social stratification, and cultural orientation) influence the style and content of the art itself. Furthermore, it is possible to take Bidesia art as an enterprise of aesthetics, so that it can be analysed and experienced purely in terms of its entertainment or pleasure value. Bidesia art form which has often been understood as resistant and carrying the potential to change mentalities and thereby societies, that can also be understood as propagandist. This chapter mainly put forth's about the predicaments of the corresponding village life, rather than reflecting a process of change or challenging the dominant values.

Indeed, the reviews about Bidesia art reflect the very manner in which any work can be understood as propagandist.

Bhikhari Thakur who configured Bidesia art was a bhojpuri public poet in reality.Bhojpuri people see the aspects of good and bad things about their lives in Bidesia folk where the issues pertaining rural life have been depicted beautifully.(Dr. Uday Narayan Tiwari in 'Bhojpuri Bhasha aur Sahitya' PP.44-45)

Bidesia art became very famous mainly because of it's emphasis on people's everyday life. Bhikhari Thakur's Bidesia art alone popularized Bhojpuri more than anybody and anything else. Thakur's Bidesia art through his bhojpuri plays successfully campaigned for the Bhojpuri language in the Bhojpuri speaking area.(Dr. Krishnadev Upadhyay in'Bhojpuri Sahitya ka Itihas' PP.409).

Accordingly, this chapter seeks to analyse some of the literature produced in Eastern Uttar Pradesh and Bihar by Bhikhari Thakur. Thakur's well known works are mainly in the form of plays which also become the main constituent of Bidesia art. The aim of this chapter is to contextualise Thakur's literature as main constituent of Bidesia form in their social contexts.

the director of Bidesia art Bhikhari Thakur was born in 1887 in a small village in Chapra district of Bihar. Thakur was a barber by caste and came from a very poor family. Thakur was a poet, lyricist, playwright, play director, folk musician and an actor at the same time. He was equally artful in all these creative fields. He successfully embraced attributes of the traditional form of theatrical presentations but at the same time, did not delay any in bringing about improvisations when the situation demanded. The main themes of Bidesia art revolved around the relevant issues of the existing society. The medium of dialogue in this art is mainly in the form of poetry, but in order to make it more interesting and entertaining, besides, there is use of easy colloquial language. He did not design his stage according to the conventional norms. stage used for Bidesia art used to be open from three sides and very simple, generally in the form of a raised rectangular platform. One side was covered with the tent sheet. The most important characteristic of this art thus turn out to be it's dialogic nature. This kept people involved and interested.

This was perhaps the first experiment of this kind in any theatrical style in India (Singh, 2005). It did not opt the norm of theatre as being a building where people entered and positioned in a predesigned way to witness the theatre spaces. It reminded constantly that theatre was a public act. A dialectic between traditions and conventions and the challenges of contemporary world gave rise to new experiments and made this art dynamic. Moreover, the main tendency positioned in this art was social issues raised through entertainment.

Bidesia art lead us through the many layers of India's rural & agrarian society, giving an insight into their tribulations, philosophy towards life and difficult circumstances under whose ascending pressure Bidesia became an art form and Thakur, an established writer and a theatre person. He belonged to the lower section of the society. he was a barber(naai) and had access to the women's world during certain rituals. this very fact forms the basis from which all his creative endeavour took off (Upadhyay, 1972). The times when Bidesia as an art form originates were full of political, social, economic turmoil. In the turbulent period of India's struggle for freedom. Bidesia art took up the cause of the deserted,crucified and disturbed women of rural India. This proved to be the starting point in the establishment of Bidesia folk genre as an art form. For Thakur, the liberation of India as a country had an equal and parallel meaning in the rescue of the rural women from their hardships. Having predicted this in Bidesia art, Bhikhari Thakur fought relentlessly for the cause of women discarded by their husbands in search of a livelihood to bigger cities and towns and the brutal practice of selling young girls to older men on the pretext of marriage (Singh,2005). In spite of impoverished and deprived circumstances, 'Bidesia' managed to become a famous art form (Singh,2005).

Brief Background to Bidesia art form:

Bidesia art was very much affected by the social movements of Bengal. Bhikhri thakur has thinly examined the disagreements tenacious in his own society after coming back from Calcutta (present day Kolkata). through Bidesia art form, He has successfully endeavoured to deepen the issues around economy, religion, caste and gender based exploitation. This chapter is an attempt to locate the element of political in Bidesia art as a realm created by the whole performing paraphernalia of this art in general, huge viewership and the socially relevant issues raised in particular. Here by, there is a clear employment to articulate Jacques Rancier's argument (as mentioned earlier) on the political.

Bidesia theatre attracted and pulled huge audiences especially when performed by Bhikhari Thakur and his acting troupe. Thakur composed many popular Bidesia plays which were filled with songs based on folk tunes such as *lorihayan, jantsari, sorthi, birha, barahmasa, chaupayi etc.* Thakur's first play known as *Bidesia*, is one of the most famous plays in Eastern UP and Bihar. Bhikhari's immense popularity in this region makes him a minor legend. (Bhikhari Thakur Rachnavali, 2005). There are hundreds of natak companies in Eastern UP and Bihar who call themselves as 'Bidesia style natak companies' and they are very popular in the area (Upadhyay, 1972).

The popularity of Bidesia art form was due to the description of common events and experiences, related to the pain of migration, a theme that touched a common chord in the Bhojpuri audience. The combination of comic relief and satire on the existing system also established Bidesia theatre as an extremely popular form of folk art and culture. These plays were also a statement on the existing social dichotomies like exploitation based on class, caste, gender and process of displacements of the Bhojpuri migrants (Tiwari, 2005)

Bidesia art is a product of the analysis of the lives of women, their social condition and psychology in the existing rural setting. Bidesia art elucidate many aspects of women's lives for instance, by looking at the life of a young girl in the plays *Beti Viyog* (The separated daughter) and *Nand Bhojai*. He looked at the lives of married women, in his plays, *Bhai Virodh, Ganga Snan, Putra Vadh*, and women with migrant husbands in the plays *Bidesia, Vidhwa*.

In the play *Gabar Gichor*, there is an urge to show very clearly about the radical move opted by a woman. Thakur created a very radical character of a desi style woman vis a vis norms of patriarchal social structure whose migrant husband does not return for fifteen years. In between she develops a physical relation with another man and gives birth to a child. Despite a lot of accusations and exploitation, she successfully fights and takes care of her child. Thakur through Bidesia art seems to be fighting for the rescue of women and the wish to bring up their children.

As mentioned before, this is not to say that Bidesia art did not conform to the understood norms of the society. Through this art form, he glorified the status of women as mothers and virtuous daughters-in-law. In the play

Ganga Snan, he is very critical about the character of the daughter-in-law and almost portrays her as a disrespectful woman, keeping in mind her behaviour towards her mother-in-law. In the play *Putra Vadh*, he focused on the affection of *Badki* (name of the mother) towards her son *Chetram*. In the play *Bidesia*, he talked about the problem of prostitution as a social problem and also suggested ways for the rehabilitation of sex workers.

Bhikhari Thakur was a barbar by caste and his own life as one member of the underclass showed the day-to-day challenges of this class. Perhaps, the most important aim of this folk art was to create an awareness about these contradictions in the lives of the underclass and also suggest ways to get rid of these miseries.

As mentioned earlier, The key issues that Bidesia art dealt with were child-marriage, uneven marriages (young girl married to an old man), selling off daughters for wealth, families getting nuclear in a lust of wealth and property, crime, addiction, theft, gambling etc. The result of these plays was felt very soon and selling of daughters for wealth was criticised and looked down upon by everyone. Widow remarriage was promoted and incidentally, during the same period, child marriage was banned by the government (Singh, 2005). this argument very well supports my assumption on culture in Bidesia art.

As talked about before, The names of the characters used in this art also came from the Dalit and other lower caste communities, e.g. *Updar Udwas, Jhatul, Chitru* etc. as during this time, Dalits and other lower castes usually did not have names like other upper caste names. The other important fact here is that, most of his actors belonged to the lower castes. Therefore, it can be assumed here that, Bidesia art incorporated all encouraging steps and made every positive attempt for the development and appraisal of the Dalit and lower caste communities (Tiwari, 2005).

Bidesia art reflects the system of various ideas on which the contemporary society was organised. As it as become very clear that sometimes it conforms to the societal values and norms of the feudal, patriarchal society, especially in the plays Bidesia and Kalyug Prem, where there is an act that a woman should be chaste to her husband and take care of the family, household and children. Thus this art also keeps falling back to the same kind of false consciousness that it constantly tried to separate from.

Although, it is clear that Bidesia art is disseminating for women's destitution. But at the same time it also fights for the freedom of women and their sexual rights in the play *Gabarghichor.* If we bring in the base and superstructure model here, then we can see that this kind of art is a result of the economic base. Since

Bhikhari came from a backward caste family, he was too poor to lead his life in a normal way. The social and economic conditions, pressurised, relocate and earn his living (Singh, 2005). So, he had lived through all these hardships, ill-treatment, brought about by the dominant classes and produced a work, which in a way, are rated against the contemporary social practices. Since all his plays directly talk about the lower castes, deprived class His theatre troop was also mainly comprised of dalits and lower caste people (Bhikhari Thakur Rachnavali). The names of the characters in this art form are also dalit and lower caste names. According to Macherey, literature and art support to ideological communications. Bidesia art along the same line, has definitely provided some kind of ideological communication. The selling of daughters for wealth was considered to be a matter of truncated reputation and crime. The Government of India also banned child marriages during the same period (Singh, 2005). The subject matter of Bidesia art was influenced by the social practices and Thakur wanted people to know about their problems. He can be seen as propagating a kind of consciousness among people through this art form which comes close to what Luckacs meant when he talked about socialist realism as a perfect form of creativity, where the writer gets first hand information, lives it, and produces authentic arguments (As mentioned earlier).

Accordingly, a certain aesthetic organization of sense experience. Based on the above discussion, it can be said that Bidesia art made an impact in the field of the political through its performance. but it looks like certain that this art is primarily a form of entertainment. it falls mainly in the purview of culture and gets viewed primarily throgh aesthetic sense. Besides, it contained a system of ideas which some times conformed to the societal values and sometimes moved away from them.

Bidesia art form configures stages, demonstrates and rallies around notions of shared belief systems, ultimate values and common culture, as the mainstay of social order in the contemporary semi-feudal societies of eastern Uttar Pradesh and western part of Bihar. The element of political in Bidesia art form gets reflected in the way it successfully propagates about the pains and sorrows of the common masses. This propagation gets articulated as a critique to dominant ideology that functions to incorporate common masses into the society of the ruling class, thereby maintaining social cohesion. Bidesia art form through Bhojpuri plays and songs can be seen combating this very false consciousness offering a critique to the semi-feudal structure of Bhojpuri society and also the existing class relations. Plays and songs of Bidesia art form gain popularity mostly by their aesthetic attributes. Working within the domain of sociology of literature, the basic concern throughout this chapter is to point out this simultaneous politico-cultural and aesthetic dimension of Bhojpuri 'Bidesia' art form. This assertion is collaborated through the very understanding of the terms politics and aesthetics forwarded in this chapter. Politics according to Jacques rancier (2005) is the struggle of an unrecognized party for an equal recognition in the established order. Politics, he argues itself is not the exercise of power or struggle for power. It is first of all the configuration of a space as political, the framing of a specific sphere of experience. The setting of objects show cased as 'common' and of subjects to whom the capacity is recognized to designate these objects and discuss about them. Politics first is thus the conflict about the very existence of that sphere of experience. Moreover, aesthetics is bound up in this battle, because the battle takes over the image of society what it is permissible to say or show. Bidesia art form very well incorporates the above made argument. The use the term aesthetic here in a sense close to the Kantian idea of a priori forms of sensibility (Kant 1900). Referring to the concepts of time and space as logically necessary conditions for there to be an experience at all, thus 'Bidesia' form of art is seen as both a matter of art and aesthetics and also fundamentally a matter of time and space. This is the manner in which it is possible to understand the political and cultural impulse in the aesthesis of 'Bidesia art form'. There is this argument that 'Bidesia' art form in spite of being resistant to the dominant ideologies, fall within the realm of politics and culture and also gain popularity because they carry an aesthetic appeal. In this manner, there is an attempt to restage the radical writing movement in Bhojpuri Literature as an aesthetic movement, in which the practices of the underclass, the marginalized and women were formulated first and fore most in encircling the volume to vocalized their experiences.

Conclusion

In this book I have tried to look at the relationship between society and literature in the specific context of the Bhojpuri songs, plays and poetries found in the works of Bhikhari Thakur and Gorakh Pandey. I began with addressing the idea that the works of these authors have been considered revolutionary and resistant towards the dominant ideologies as interpreted by the Marxian Theories. The dominant ideology in the Marxian sense, as mentioned, is a false consciousness diffused by the dominant classes among the masses who are thus rendered incapable of defending their own class interests.

I however tried to show in the thesis that these works, rather fall in the realm of agitation propaganda, in terms of the Russian *Agitprop* and *Prolethult* strategies. That is to say, these works can be understood as combining both agitational/political and aesthetic enterprises in the mobilization of public opinion. Indeed, this is possible because of the very nature of politics itself. Taking off from Ranciere, it is possible to understand politics as something that relies on the formation of a 'common sense' or a sensibility which the masses are familiar with. It is in this attempt to gain a common sensibility, any political activity and writing in particular relies on aestheticism. Understood in the Kantian sense, aesthetics is an a priori form of sensibility which relies not just on taste but also on time and space, that is, upon the place of both the writers and the receivers in a society. It is in this sense that any literature that attempts to be radical and resistant situates itself in the realm of propaganda art. As Ellul explained it propaganda also has an agitation motive. Although it is oppositional, it may seek to overthrow an established order, but may equally be used to address psychological barriers of habits, beliefs and judgments. Propaganda also has an integration effect that and can therefore be ineffective because it negotiates between dominant and at the same time opposing values of society. Accordingly, I have argued that the works of Pandey and Thakur in spite of being resistant to the dominant ideologies, fall within the realm of propagandist literature and also gain popularity because they carry an aesthetic appeal.

In this attempt, I began from the understanding of literature offered by Marxian Literary Theory, which sees literature as oscillating between reflecting the dominant class ideologies or false consciousness and/or trying to break away from it. In Chapter One, I undertook a review of literature of the various Marxist Theories that have reflected upon these two dimensions of literature.

Through this chapter, I could address my first objective, which was to substantiate that:

It is possible to see literature as moving away from the dominant bourgeois ideologies. Thus texts, poetries and other forms of theatrical writings can be seen as resisting the false consciousness generated by the dominant classes'[13].

Moreover, in this chapter, I also located the manner in which the Marxian theories themselves acknowledge the aesthetic potential of literature. Art does more than just passively reflect the experience. Thus, while Art is held within ideology, it also manages to distance itself from it. This distancing is done to the point where, art permits us to 'feel' and 'perceive' the ideology from which it springs.

After addressing the manner in which Marxian Literary Theory has looked at the relationship between society and literature, in Chapter Two, I look at the case of Bhikhari Thakur and the literature produced by him. I argued that although Thakur made an impact in the field of the political through his work but there is no denying the fact that his plays were primarily a form of entertainment. Besides, they contained a system of ideas which some times conformed to the societal values and sometimes deviated from them.

---

[13]   Refer to the introduction of this text..

Similarly in Chapter three, an analysis of Pandey's work brings out the manner in which the emergence of politics itself, which emerges through the antagonism of a given order, has aesthetics at its core to the extent that it can bring about a redistribution of the sensible, a shift in public consciousness concerning how we see, what is seen.

In both chapters two and three, I have looked at the manner in which it is it is possible to take literature as an enterprise of aesthetics, so that it can be analyzed and experienced purely in terms of its entertainment or pleasure value. By looking at these writings that have been often understood as resistant and carrying the potential to change mentalities and thereby societies, literary art can also be understood as propagandist. I have argued that these radical writings, rather than reflecting a process of change or challenging the dominant values, end up propagandizing the issuess at hand. Moreover, this propaganda bases itself upon the very aesthetic value of art, which is often denounced by Marxist writers. Finally, literature necessarily reflects ideas about the way in which a society is organized. It reflects the social influences of the authors and the means by which their literary products reach an audience. It tells us how the sociohistorical context (defined by historical time, economic and political structure, social stratification, and cultural orientation) influence the style and content of the authors' works. Chapter no 4 is mainly focused on the analysis and recommendation of the ideas of Aesthetics and Politics that percolate through the writings of my research subjects.

Bibliography

1.   Althusser, L. 1965. *For Marx*. London : Verso.

2.   Bakhtin,M. 1984. *Speech, Genres and other late Essays*. Austin: University of Texas Press.

3.   Bourdieu, P. 1993. *The Field of Cultural Production: Essays on Art and Literature*. Cambridge : Polity Press.

4.   Barthes, R. 1975. *The Pleasure of the Text Translated hy Richard Miller*. London : Hill and Wang.

5.   Bourdieu, P. 1996. *The Rules of Art : Genesis and Structure of the Literary Field*. California : Stanford University Press.

6.   Dalmia, V. 2006. *India's Literary History – Essays on the 10th Century*. New Delhi : Permanent Black.

7.   Dickens, C. 1838. *Oliver Twist*. London : Chapman and Hall. Eagleton, T. 1976. *Criticism and Ideology*. London : New Left Books. Eagleton,

T. 1976. *Marxism and Literary Criticism*. London : Methuen and Co. Ltd.

8.   Eagleton, T. 1976. 'Raymond Williams' Important Work. *New Left Review*, Jan-Feb 1976. 95.

9.   Ellul, J. 1973. *Propaganda: The Formation of men's attitude*. New York : Vintage Books.

10.   Foulkes, A.P. 1983. *Literature and propaganda*. London, NewYork : Metheun & Co. Ltd.

11.   Goldmann, L. 1975. *Towards Sociology of the Novel*. London : Tavistock Publications Ltd.

12.   Gramsci, A. 1977. *Selections From Political Writings, 1910- 1926*. London : Lawrence and Wishart.

13.   Griffin, Robert and Rick Tilman. 1998. *The aesthetics of Thorstein Veblen Revisited, In Cultural Dynamics 10 (Novermher 1998)*. Sage Publications Ltd. Griswold, W. 1993. Recent Move in the Sociology of Literature. *Annual Review of Sociology*, 1993, 19: 455-67.

14.   Iser, W. 1978. *The Implied Reader: Patterns of Communication in Prose Fiction from Bunyan to Beckett*. Baltimore .-Johns Hopkins University. Lenin, V.I. 1987. *Essential Works of Lenin*: "What

Is to Be Done?" and Other Writings. London : Dover Publications

15. Kant, I. 1900. *Critique of Pure Reason.* New York : Colonial Press. Lukacs, G. 1972. *Political Writings 1919-1929.* London : NLB. Macherey, P. 1989. *Theory of Literary Production.* London : Routledge. Macherey, P. 1995. *The object of Literature.* Cambridge : Cambridge University Press.

16. Marx, K. and Engels, F. 1938. *German Ideology.* London : Lawrence and Wishart. Marx, K. and Engels, F. 1970. *Communist Manifesto.* Harmondsworth : Penguin. Marx, K. and Engels, F. 1978. On *Literature and Art.* Moscow: Progressive Publication House.

17. Marx, K. 1979. A *contribution to the Critique of Political Economy.* London : International Publishers.

18. Orsini, F. 2002. *Hindi Public Sphere, 1920-1940: Language and Literature in the Age of Nationalism.* New Delhi : Oxford University Press.

19. Pandey, G. 1983. *Jagtey Raho Sone Walon.* Delhi : Radhakrishna Prakashan. Pandey, M. 2006.

Sahitya Ke Samajshastra Ki Bhoomiha. Delhi : Goyal Enterprises.

20. Plekhanov, G. 1898. *On the Alleged Crisis in Marxism*. Selected Philosophical Works in Five Volumes.

21. Prakash, A. 2002. *Approaches in Literary Theory: Marxism*. Delhi : Worldview Publications.

22. Pollock, S. 2004. *Literary Cultures in History; Reconstructions from South Asia*. New Delhi : Oxford University Press.

23. Prakash, A. 2002. *Approaches in Literary Theory: Marxism*. Delhi : Worldview Publications.

24. Pranaykrishna. 2004. *Samay Ka Pahiya; Selected Poems of Gorakh Pandey*. Mumbai, Meerut : Samwad.

25. Rai, A. 2000. *Hindi Nationalism*. Delhi : Orient Longman.

26. Ranciere, Jacques, From Politics to Aesthetics? Volume 28,

27. DOI 10.3366/para.2005.28.1.13, ISSN 0264-8334, Available Online March 2005.

28. Rose, J. 2007. *The Last Resistance*. London : Verso.

29. Singh, N. P. 2005. *Bhihhari Thakur Rachnavali.* Patna : Bihar Rashtra Bhasha Parishad.

30. Singh, N. 1991. *Karl Marx: Art and Literary Criticism.* New Delhi : Rajkamal Publications.

31. Singh, N. 2005. *Alochak he Mukh Se.* New Delhi : Rajkamal Publications.

32. Stark, U. 2007. An *Empire of Boohs : The Naval Kishore Press and the Diffusion of the Printed V/ orld in Colonial India.* New Delhi : Permanent Black.

33. Tiwari, U.N. 1983. *Bhojpuri Bhasha our Sahitya.* Patna : Bihar Rashtra Bhasha Parishad.

34. Upadhyay, K. 1972. *Bhojpuri Sahitya ha Itihas.* Varanasi : Indian Folk Culture Research Institute.

35. Valmiki, O.P. 2003. *Joothan-An Untouchable's Life.* Columbia : Columbia University Press.

36. Williams, R. 1999. *Marxism and Literature.* London : Routledge. Articles and Journals:

37. Damodaran, S. 2006. *Protest Through Music : A Documentation and Analysis of the Structure, Content and context of the Musical Tradition of*

the *IPTA*. Delhi : Independent Fellowship, Sarai, CSDS.

38. Sulabh, H. 2006. 'Batohi' in *Rang Prasang, Year 9, Issue 3, July-September.* New-Delhi : National School of Dram

Note:

    Internet sources- Wikipedia and e-books.